MOTIVATION PLAN

DATE: _____   M   T   W   TH   F   SA   SU

TO DO

☐ ....

☐ ....

☐ ....

☐ ....

WORKOUT

☐ ....

☐ ....

☐ ....

☐ ....

APPOINTMENT

☐ ....

☐ ....

☐ ....

☐ ....

MEAL PLAN

☐ ....

☐ ....

☐ ....

☐ ....

FINANCIAL GOAL

☐ ....

☐ ....

☐ ....

☐ ....

WATER INTAKE

☐ ....

☐ ....

☐ ....

☐ ....

POSITIVE MOMENT

....

....

....

....

NOTE

....

....

....

....

MOTIVATION PLAN

DATE: _____   M T W TH F SA SU

TO DO
- [ ] ....
- [ ] ....
- [ ] ....
- [ ] ....

WORKOUT
- [ ] ....
- [ ] ....
- [ ] ....
- [ ] ....

APPOINTMENT
- [ ] ....
- [ ] ....
- [ ] ....
- [ ] ....

MEAL PLAN
- [ ] ....
- [ ] ....
- [ ] ....
- [ ] ....

FINANCIAL GOAL
- [ ] ....
- [ ] ....
- [ ] ....
- [ ] ....

WATER INTAKE
- [ ] ....
- [ ] ....
- [ ] ....
- [ ] ....

POSITIVE MOMENT
....
....
....
....

NOTE
....
....
....
....

MOTIVATION PLAN

DATE: _____   M T W TH F SA SU

TO DO

☐ ....
☐ ....
☐ ....
☐ ....

WORKOUT

☐ ....
☐ ....
☐ ....
☐ ....

APPOINTMENT

☐ ....
☐ ....
☐ ....
☐ ....

MEAL PLAN

☐ ....
☐ ....
☐ ....
☐ ....

FINANCIAL GOAL

☐ ....
☐ ....
☐ ....
☐ ....

WATER INTAKE

☐ ....
☐ ....
☐ ....
☐ ....

POSITIVE MOMENT

....
....
....
....

NOTE

....
....
....
....

MOTIVATION PLAN

DATE: _____   M   T   W   TH   F   SA   SU

TO DO

☐ ....

☐ ....

☐ ....

☐ ....

WORKOUT

☐ ....

☐ ....

☐ ....

☐ ....

APPOINTMENT

☐ ....

☐ ....

☐ ....

☐ ....

MEAL PLAN

☐ ....

☐ ....

☐ ....

☐ ....

FINANCIAL GOAL

☐ ....

☐ ....

☐ ....

☐ ....

WATER INTAKE

☐ ....

☐ ....

☐ ....

☐ ....

POSITIVE MOMENT

....

....

....

....

NOTE

....

....

....

....

MOTIVATION PLAN

DATE: _____   M T W TH F SA SU

TO DO
- ☐ ....
- ☐ ....
- ☐ ....
- ☐ ....

WORKOUT
- ☐ ....
- ☐ ....
- ☐ ....
- ☐ ....

APPOINTMENT
- ☐ ....
- ☐ ....
- ☐ ....
- ☐ ....

MEAL PLAN
- ☐ ....
- ☐ ....
- ☐ ....
- ☐ ....

FINANCIAL GOAL
- ☐ ....
- ☐ ....
- ☐ ....
- ☐ ....

WATER INTAKE
- ☐ ....
- ☐ ....
- ☐ ....
- ☐ ....

POSITIVE MOMENT
....
....
....
....

NOTE
....
....
....
....

MOTIVATION PLAN

DATE: _____   M T W TH F SA SU

TO DO
- [ ] ....
- [ ] ....
- [ ] ....
- [ ] ....

WORKOUT
- [ ] ....
- [ ] ....
- [ ] ....
- [ ] ....

APPOINTMENT
- [ ] ....
- [ ] ....
- [ ] ....
- [ ] ....

MEAL PLAN
- [ ] ....
- [ ] ....
- [ ] ....
- [ ] ....

FINANCIAL GOAL
- [ ] ....
- [ ] ....
- [ ] ....
- [ ] ....

WATER INTAKE
- [ ] ....
- [ ] ....
- [ ] ....
- [ ] ....

POSITIVE MOMENT
....
....
....
....

NOTE
....
....
....
....

MOTIVATION PLAN

DATE: _____

M T W TH F SA SU

TO DO

- [ ] ....
- [ ] ....
- [ ] ....
- [ ] ....

WORKOUT

- [ ] ....
- [ ] ....
- [ ] ....
- [ ] ....

APPOINTMENT

- [ ] ....
- [ ] ....
- [ ] ....
- [ ] ....

MEAL PLAN

- [ ] ....
- [ ] ....
- [ ] ....
- [ ] ....

FINANCIAL GOAL

- [ ] ....
- [ ] ....
- [ ] ....
- [ ] ....

WATER INTAKE

- [ ] ....
- [ ] ....
- [ ] ....
- [ ] ....

POSITIVE MOMENT

....
....
....
....

NOTE

....
....
....
....

MOTIVATION PLAN

DATE: _____   M T W TH F SA SU

TO DO
- [ ] ....
- [ ] ....
- [ ] ....
- [ ] ....

WORKOUT
- [ ] ....
- [ ] ....
- [ ] ....
- [ ] ....

APPOINTMENT
- [ ] ....
- [ ] ....
- [ ] ....
- [ ] ....

MEAL PLAN
- [ ] ....
- [ ] ....
- [ ] ....
- [ ] ....

FINANCIAL GOAL
- [ ] ....
- [ ] ....
- [ ] ....
- [ ] ....

WATER INTAKE
- [ ] ....
- [ ] ....
- [ ] ....
- [ ] ....

POSITIVE MOMENT
....
....
....
....

NOTE
....
....
....
....

MOTIVATION PLAN

DATE: _____   M T W TH F SA SU

TO DO
- [ ] ....
- [ ] ....
- [ ] ....
- [ ] ....

WORKOUT
- [ ] ....
- [ ] ....
- [ ] ....
- [ ] ....

APPOINTMENT
- [ ] ....
- [ ] ....
- [ ] ....
- [ ] ....

MEAL PLAN
- [ ] ....
- [ ] ....
- [ ] ....
- [ ] ....

FINANCIAL GOAL
- [ ] ....
- [ ] ....
- [ ] ....
- [ ] ....

WATER INTAKE
- [ ] ....
- [ ] ....
- [ ] ....
- [ ] ....

POSITIVE MOMENT
....
....
....
....

NOTE
....
....
....
....

MOTIVATION PLAN

DATE: _____   M T W TH F SA SU

TO DO
- ☐ ....
- ☐ ....
- ☐ ....
- ☐ ....

WORKOUT
- ☐ ....
- ☐ ....
- ☐ ....
- ☐ ....

APPOINTMENT
- ☐ ....
- ☐ ....
- ☐ ....
- ☐ ....

MEAL PLAN
- ☐ ....
- ☐ ....
- ☐ ....
- ☐ ....

FINANCIAL GOAL
- ☐ ....
- ☐ ....
- ☐ ....
- ☐ ....

WATER INTAKE
- ☐ ....
- ☐ ....
- ☐ ....
- ☐ ....

POSITIVE MOMENT
....
....
....
....

NOTE
....
....
....
....

MOTIVATION PLAN

DATE: _____   M T W TH F SA SU

TO DO

☐ ....
☐ ....
☐ ....
☐ ....

WORKOUT

☐ ....
☐ ....
☐ ....
☐ ....

APPOINTMENT

☐ ....
☐ ....
☐ ....
☐ ....

MEAL PLAN

☐ ....
☐ ....
☐ ....
☐ ....

FINANCIAL GOAL

☐ ....
☐ ....
☐ ....
☐ ....

WATER INTAKE

☐ ....
☐ ....
☐ ....
☐ ....

POSITIVE MOMENT

....
....
....
....

NOTE

....
....
....
....

MOTIVATION PLAN

DATE: _____   M T W TH F SA SU

TO DO

☐ ....

☐ ....

☐ ....

☐ ....

WORKOUT

☐ ....

☐ ....

☐ ....

☐ ....

APPOINTMENT

☐ ....

☐ ....

☐ ....

☐ ....

MEAL PLAN

☐ ....

☐ ....

☐ ....

☐ ....

FINANCIAL GOAL

☐ ....

☐ ....

☐ ....

☐ ....

WATER INTAKE

☐ ....

☐ ....

☐ ....

☐ ....

POSITIVE MOMENT

....

....

....

....

NOTE

....

....

....

....

MOTIVATION PLAN

DATE: _____   M T W TH F SA SU

TO DO

☐ ....

☐ ....

☐ ....

☐ ....

WORKOUT

☐ ....

☐ ....

☐ ....

☐ ....

APPOINTMENT

☐ ....

☐ ....

☐ ....

☐ ....

MEAL PLAN

☐ ....

☐ ....

☐ ....

☐ ....

FINANCIAL GOAL

☐ ....

☐ ....

☐ ....

☐ ....

WATER INTAKE

☐ ....

☐ ....

☐ ....

☐ ....

POSITIVE MOMENT

....

....

....

....

NOTE

....

....

....

....

MOTIVATION PLAN

DATE: _____

M T W TH F SA SU

TO DO

☐ ....
☐ ....
☐ ....
☐ ....

WORKOUT

☐ ....
☐ ....
☐ ....
☐ ....

APPOINTMENT

☐ ....
☐ ....
☐ ....
☐ ....

MEAL PLAN

☐ ....
☐ ....
☐ ....
☐ ....

FINANCIAL GOAL

☐ ....
☐ ....
☐ ....
☐ ....

WATER INTAKE

☐ ....
☐ ....
☐ ....
☐ ....

POSITIVE MOMENT

....
....
....
....

NOTE

....
....
....
....

MOTIVATION PLAN

DATE: _____   M T W TH F SA SU

TO DO

☐ ....
☐ ....
☐ ....
☐ ....

WORKOUT

☐ ....
☐ ....
☐ ....
☐ ....

APPOINTMENT

☐ ....
☐ ....
☐ ....
☐ ....

MEAL PLAN

☐ ....
☐ ....
☐ ....
☐ ....

FINANCIAL GOAL

☐ ....
☐ ....
☐ ....
☐ ....

WATER INTAKE

☐ ....
☐ ....
☐ ....
☐ ....

POSITIVE MOMENT

....
....
....
....

NOTE

....
....
....
....

MOTIVATION PLAN

DATE: _____   M T W TH F SA SU

TO DO
- [ ] ....
- [ ] ....
- [ ] ....
- [ ] ....

WORKOUT
- [ ] ....
- [ ] ....
- [ ] ....
- [ ] ....

APPOINTMENT
- [ ] ....
- [ ] ....
- [ ] ....
- [ ] ....

MEAL PLAN
- [ ] ....
- [ ] ....
- [ ] ....
- [ ] ....

FINANCIAL GOAL
- [ ] ....
- [ ] ....
- [ ] ....
- [ ] ....

WATER INTAKE
- [ ] ....
- [ ] ....
- [ ] ....
- [ ] ....

POSITIVE MOMENT
....
....
....
....

NOTE
....
....
....
....

MOTIVATION PLAN

DATE: _____   M T W TH F SA SU

TO DO
- ☐ ....
- ☐ ....
- ☐ ....
- ☐ ....

WORKOUT
- ☐ ....
- ☐ ....
- ☐ ....
- ☐ ....

APPOINTMENT
- ☐ ....
- ☐ ....
- ☐ ....
- ☐ ....

MEAL PLAN
- ☐ ....
- ☐ ....
- ☐ ....
- ☐ ....

FINANCIAL GOAL
- ☐ ....
- ☐ ....
- ☐ ....
- ☐ ....

WATER INTAKE
- ☐ ....
- ☐ ....
- ☐ ....
- ☐ ....

POSITIVE MOMENT
....
....
....
....

NOTE
....
....
....
....

MOTIVATION PLAN

DATE: _____   M T W TH F SA SU

TO DO

☐ ....
☐ ....
☐ ....
☐ ....

WORKOUT

☐ ....
☐ ....
☐ ....
☐ ....

APPOINTMENT

☐ ....
☐ ....
☐ ....
☐ ....

MEAL PLAN

☐ ....
☐ ....
☐ ....
☐ ....

FINANCIAL GOAL

☐ ....
☐ ....
☐ ....
☐ ....

WATER INTAKE

☐ ....
☐ ....
☐ ....
☐ ....

POSITIVE MOMENT

....
....
....
....

NOTE

....
....
....
....

MOTIVATION PLAN

DATE: _____   M T W TH F SA SU

TO DO

- [ ] ....
- [ ] ....
- [ ] ....
- [ ] ....

WORKOUT

- [ ] ....
- [ ] ....
- [ ] ....
- [ ] ....

APPOINTMENT

- [ ] ....
- [ ] ....
- [ ] ....
- [ ] ....

MEAL PLAN

- [ ] ....
- [ ] ....
- [ ] ....
- [ ] ....

FINANCIAL GOAL

- [ ] ....
- [ ] ....
- [ ] ....
- [ ] ....

WATER INTAKE

- [ ] ....
- [ ] ....
- [ ] ....
- [ ] ....

POSITIVE MOMENT

....
....
....
....

NOTE

....
....
....
....

MOTIVATION PLAN

DATE: _____   M T W TH F SA SU

TO DO
- ☐ ....
- ☐ ....
- ☐ ....
- ☐ ....

WORKOUT
- ☐ ....
- ☐ ....
- ☐ ....
- ☐ ....

APPOINTMENT
- ☐ ....
- ☐ ....
- ☐ ....
- ☐ ....

MEAL PLAN
- ☐ ....
- ☐ ....
- ☐ ....
- ☐ ....

FINANCIAL GOAL
- ☐ ....
- ☐ ....
- ☐ ....
- ☐ ....

WATER INTAKE
- ☐ ....
- ☐ ....
- ☐ ....
- ☐ ....

POSITIVE MOMENT
....
....
....
....

NOTE
....
....
....
....

MOTIVATION PLAN

DATE: _____

M T W TH F SA SU

TO DO
- [ ] ....
- [ ] ....
- [ ] ....
- [ ] ....

WORKOUT
- [ ] ....
- [ ] ....
- [ ] ....
- [ ] ....

APPOINTMENT
- [ ] ....
- [ ] ....
- [ ] ....
- [ ] ....

MEAL PLAN
- [ ] ....
- [ ] ....
- [ ] ....
- [ ] ....

FINANCIAL GOAL
- [ ] ....
- [ ] ....
- [ ] ....
- [ ] ....

WATER INTAKE
- [ ] ....
- [ ] ....
- [ ] ....
- [ ] ....

POSITIVE MOMENT
....
....
....
....

NOTE
....
....
....
....

MOTIVATION PLAN

DATE: _____   M T W TH F SA SU

TO DO
- ☐ ....
- ☐ ....
- ☐ ....
- ☐ ....

WORKOUT
- ☐ ....
- ☐ ....
- ☐ ....
- ☐ ....

APPOINTMENT
- ☐ ....
- ☐ ....
- ☐ ....
- ☐ ....

MEAL PLAN
- ☐ ....
- ☐ ....
- ☐ ....
- ☐ ....

FINANCIAL GOAL
- ☐ ....
- ☐ ....
- ☐ ....
- ☐ ....

WATER INTAKE
- ☐ ....
- ☐ ....
- ☐ ....
- ☐ ....

POSITIVE MOMENT
....
....
....
....

NOTE
....
....
....
....

MOTIVATION PLAN

DATE: _____

M T W TH F SA SU

TO DO
- ☐
- ☐
- ☐
- ☐

WORKOUT
- ☐
- ☐
- ☐
- ☐

APPOINTMENT
- ☐
- ☐
- ☐

MEAL PLAN
- ☐
- ☐
- ☐

FINANCIAL GOAL
- ☐
- ☐
- ☐
- ☐

WATER INTAKE
- ☐
- ☐
- ☐
- ☐

POSITIVE MOMENT

NOTE

MOTIVATION PLAN

DATE: _____   M T W TH F SA SU

TO DO
- ☐ ....
- ☐ ....
- ☐ ....
- ☐ ....

WORKOUT
- ☐ ....
- ☐ ....
- ☐ ....
- ☐ ....

APPOINTMENT
- ☐ ....
- ☐ ....
- ☐ ....
- ☐ ....

MEAL PLAN
- ☐ ....
- ☐ ....
- ☐ ....
- ☐ ....

FINANCIAL GOAL
- ☐ ....
- ☐ ....
- ☐ ....
- ☐ ....

WATER INTAKE
- ☐ ....
- ☐ ....
- ☐ ....
- ☐ ....

POSITIVE MOMENT
....
....
....
....

NOTE
....
....
....
....

MOTIVATION PLAN

DATE: _____   M T W TH F SA SU

TO DO

- ☐ ....
- ☐ ....
- ☐ ....
- ☐ ....

WORKOUT

- ☐ ....
- ☐ ....
- ☐ ....
- ☐ ....

APPOINTMENT

- ☐ ....
- ☐ ....
- ☐ ....
- ☐ ....

MEAL PLAN

- ☐ ....
- ☐ ....
- ☐ ....
- ☐ ....

FINANCIAL GOAL

- ☐ ....
- ☐ ....
- ☐ ....
- ☐ ....

WATER INTAKE

- ☐ ....
- ☐ ....
- ☐ ....
- ☐ ....

POSITIVE MOMENT

....
....
....
....

NOTE

....
....
....
....

MOTIVATION PLAN

DATE: _____   M   T   W   TH   F   SA   SU

TO DO

- [ ] ....
- [ ] ....
- [ ] ....
- [ ] ....

WORKOUT

- [ ] ....
- [ ] ....
- [ ] ....
- [ ] ....

APPOINTMENT

- [ ] ....
- [ ] ....
- [ ] ....
- [ ] ....

MEAL PLAN

- [ ] ....
- [ ] ....
- [ ] ....
- [ ] ....

FINANCIAL GOAL

- [ ] ....
- [ ] ....
- [ ] ....
- [ ] ....

WATER INTAKE

- [ ] ....
- [ ] ....
- [ ] ....
- [ ] ....

POSITIVE MOMENT

....
....
....
....

NOTE

....
....
....
....

MOTIVATION PLAN

DATE: _____

M T W TH F SA SU

TO DO

- ☐ ....
- ☐ ....
- ☐ ....
- ☐ ....

WORKOUT

- ☐ ....
- ☐ ....
- ☐ ....
- ☐ ....

APPOINTMENT

- ☐ ....
- ☐ ....
- ☐ ....
- ☐ ....

MEAL PLAN

- ☐ ....
- ☐ ....
- ☐ ....
- ☐ ....

FINANCIAL GOAL

- ☐ ....
- ☐ ....
- ☐ ....
- ☐ ....

WATER INTAKE

- ☐ ....
- ☐ ....
- ☐ ....
- ☐ ....

POSITIVE MOMENT

....
....
....
....

NOTE

....
....
....
....

MOTIVATION PLAN

DATE: _____   M T W TH F SA SU

TO DO
- [ ] ....
- [ ] ....
- [ ] ....
- [ ] ....

WORKOUT
- [ ] ....
- [ ] ....
- [ ] ....
- [ ] ....

APPOINTMENT
- [ ] ....
- [ ] ....
- [ ] ....
- [ ] ....

MEAL PLAN
- [ ] ....
- [ ] ....
- [ ] ....
- [ ] ....

FINANCIAL GOAL
- [ ] ....
- [ ] ....
- [ ] ....
- [ ] ....

WATER INTAKE
- [ ] ....
- [ ] ....
- [ ] ....
- [ ] ....

POSITIVE MOMENT
....
....
....
....

NOTE
....
....
....
....

MOTIVATION PLAN

DATE: _____   M T W TH F SA SU

TO DO
- ☐ ....
- ☐ ....
- ☐ ....
- ☐ ....

WORKOUT
- ☐ ....
- ☐ ....
- ☐ ....
- ☐ ....

APPOINTMENT
- ☐ ....
- ☐ ....
- ☐ ....
- ☐ ....

MEAL PLAN
- ☐ ....
- ☐ ....
- ☐ ....
- ☐ ....

FINANCIAL GOAL
- ☐ ....
- ☐ ....
- ☐ ....
- ☐ ....

WATER INTAKE
- ☐ ....
- ☐ ....
- ☐ ....
- ☐ ....

POSITIVE MOMENT
....
....
....
....

NOTE
....
....
....
....

MOTIVATION PLAN

DATE: _____   M   T   W   TH   F   SA   SU

TO DO
☐ ....
☐ ....
☐ ....
☐ ....

WORKOUT
☐ ....
☐ ....
☐ ....
☐ ....

APPOINTMENT
☐ ....
☐ ....
☐ ....
☐ ....

MEAL PLAN
☐ ....
☐ ....
☐ ....
☐ ....

FINANCIAL GOAL
☐ ....
☐ ....
☐ ....
☐ ....

WATER INTAKE
☐ ....
☐ ....
☐ ....
☐ ....

POSITIVE MOMENT
....
....
....
....

NOTE
....
....
....
....

MOTIVATION PLAN

DATE: _____   M T W TH F SA SU

TO DO
- ☐
- ☐
- ☐
- ☐

WORKOUT
- ☐
- ☐
- ☐
- ☐

APPOINTMENT
- ☐
- ☐
- ☐
- ☐

MEAL PLAN
- ☐
- ☐
- ☐
- ☐

FINANCIAL GOAL
- ☐
- ☐
- ☐
- ☐

WATER INTAKE
- ☐
- ☐
- ☐
- ☐

POSITIVE MOMENT

NOTE

MOTIVATION PLAN

DATE: _____   M   T   W   TH   F   SA   SU

TO DO

☐ ....

☐ ....

☐ ....

☐ ....

WORKOUT

☐ ....

☐ ....

☐ ....

☐ ....

APPOINTMENT

☐ ....

☐ ....

☐ ....

☐ ....

MEAL PLAN

☐ ....

☐ ....

☐ ....

☐ ....

FINANCIAL GOAL

☐ ....

☐ ....

☐ ....

☐ ....

WATER INTAKE

☐ ....

☐ ....

☐ ....

☐ ....

POSITIVE MOMENT

....

....

....

....

NOTE

....

....

....

....

MOTIVATION PLAN

DATE: _____   M T W TH F SA SU

TO DO
- [ ]
- [ ]
- [ ]
- [ ]

WORKOUT
- [ ]
- [ ]
- [ ]
- [ ]

APPOINTMENT
- [ ]
- [ ]
- [ ]
- [ ]

MEAL PLAN
- [ ]
- [ ]
- [ ]
- [ ]

FINANCIAL GOAL
- [ ]
- [ ]
- [ ]
- [ ]

WATER INTAKE
- [ ]
- [ ]
- [ ]
- [ ]

POSITIVE MOMENT

NOTE

MOTIVATION PLAN

DATE: _____   M T W TH F SA SU

TO DO
- [ ] ....
- [ ] ....
- [ ] ....
- [ ] ....

WORKOUT
- [ ] ....
- [ ] ....
- [ ] ....
- [ ] ....

APPOINTMENT
- [ ] ....
- [ ] ....
- [ ] ....
- [ ] ....

MEAL PLAN
- [ ] ....
- [ ] ....
- [ ] ....
- [ ] ....

FINANCIAL GOAL
- [ ] ....
- [ ] ....
- [ ] ....
- [ ] ....

WATER INTAKE
- [ ] ....
- [ ] ....
- [ ] ....
- [ ] ....

POSITIVE MOMENT
....
....
....
....

NOTE
....
....
....
....

MOTIVATION PLAN

DATE: _____   M T W TH F SA SU

TO DO
- [ ] ....
- [ ] ....
- [ ] ....
- [ ] ....

WORKOUT
- [ ] ....
- [ ] ....
- [ ] ....
- [ ] ....

APPOINTMENT
- [ ] ....
- [ ] ....
- [ ] ....
- [ ] ....

MEAL PLAN
- [ ] ....
- [ ] ....
- [ ] ....
- [ ] ....

FINANCIAL GOAL
- [ ] ....
- [ ] ....
- [ ] ....
- [ ] ....

WATER INTAKE
- [ ] ....
- [ ] ....
- [ ] ....
- [ ] ....

POSITIVE MOMENT
....
....
....
....

NOTE
....
....
....
....

MOTIVATION PLAN

DATE: _____   M T W TH F SA SU

TO DO
- [ ] ....
- [ ] ....
- [ ] ....
- [ ] ....

WORKOUT
- [ ] ....
- [ ] ....
- [ ] ....
- [ ] ....

APPOINTMENT
- [ ] ....
- [ ] ....
- [ ] ....
- [ ] ....

MEAL PLAN
- [ ] ....
- [ ] ....
- [ ] ....
- [ ] ....

FINANCIAL GOAL
- [ ] ....
- [ ] ....
- [ ] ....
- [ ] ....

WATER INTAKE
- [ ] ....
- [ ] ....
- [ ] ....
- [ ] ....

POSITIVE MOMENT
....
....
....
....

NOTE
....
....
....
....

MOTIVATION PLAN

DATE: _____   M T W TH F SA SU

TO DO
- ☐ ....
- ☐ ....
- ☐ ....
- ☐ ....

WORKOUT
- ☐ ....
- ☐ ....
- ☐ ....
- ☐ ....

APPOINTMENT
- ☐ ....
- ☐ ....
- ☐ ....
- ☐ ....

MEAL PLAN
- ☐ ....
- ☐ ....
- ☐ ....

FINANCIAL GOAL
- ☐ ....
- ☐ ....
- ☐ ....
- ☐ ....

WATER INTAKE
- ☐ ....
- ☐ ....
- ☐ ....
- ☐ ....

POSITIVE MOMENT
....
....
....
....

NOTE
....
....
....
....

MOTIVATION PLAN

DATE: _____   M   T   W   TH   F   SA   SU

TO DO

☐ ....

☐ ....

☐ ....

☐ ....

WORKOUT

☐ ....

☐ ....

☐ ....

☐ ....

APPOINTMENT

☐ ....

☐ ....

☐ ....

☐ ....

MEAL PLAN

☐ ....

☐ ....

☐ ....

☐ ....

FINANCIAL GOAL

☐ ....

☐ ....

☐ ....

☐ ....

WATER INTAKE

☐ ....

☐ ....

☐ ....

☐ ....

POSITIVE MOMENT

....

....

....

....

NOTE

....

....

....

....

MOTIVATION PLAN

DATE: _____

M T W TH F SA SU

TO DO

- [ ] ....
- [ ] ....
- [ ] ....
- [ ] ....

WORKOUT

- [ ] ....
- [ ] ....
- [ ] ....
- [ ] ....

APPOINTMENT

- [ ] ....
- [ ] ....
- [ ] ....
- [ ] ....

MEAL PLAN

- [ ] ....
- [ ] ....
- [ ] ....
- [ ] ....

FINANCIAL GOAL

- [ ] ....
- [ ] ....
- [ ] ....
- [ ] ....

WATER INTAKE

- [ ] ....
- [ ] ....
- [ ] ....
- [ ] ....

POSITIVE MOMENT

....
....
....
....

NOTE

....
....
....
....

MOTIVATION PLAN

DATE: _____   M T W TH F SA SU

TO DO
- ☐ ....
- ☐ ....
- ☐ ....
- ☐ ....

WORKOUT
- ☐ ....
- ☐ ....
- ☐ ....
- ☐ ....

APPOINTMENT
- ☐ ....
- ☐ ....
- ☐ ....
- ☐ ....

MEAL PLAN
- ☐ ....
- ☐ ....
- ☐ ....
- ☐ ....

FINANCIAL GOAL
- ☐ ....
- ☐ ....
- ☐ ....
- ☐ ....

WATER INTAKE
- ☐ ....
- ☐ ....
- ☐ ....
- ☐ ....

POSITIVE MOMENT
....
....
....
....

NOTE
....
....
....
....

MOTIVATION PLAN

DATE: _____   M T W TH F SA SU

TO DO

- ☐ ....
- ☐ ....
- ☐ ....
- ☐ ....

WORKOUT

- ☐ ....
- ☐ ....
- ☐ ....
- ☐ ....

APPOINTMENT

- ☐ ....
- ☐ ....
- ☐ ....
- ☐ ....

MEAL PLAN

- ☐ ....
- ☐ ....
- ☐ ....
- ☐ ....

FINANCIAL GOAL

- ☐ ....
- ☐ ....
- ☐ ....
- ☐ ....

WATER INTAKE

- ☐ ....
- ☐ ....
- ☐ ....
- ☐ ....

POSITIVE MOMENT

....
....
....
....

NOTE

....
....
....
....

MOTIVATION PLAN

DATE: _____   M T W TH F SA SU

TO DO	WORKOUT
☐	☐
☐	☐
☐	☐
☐	☐

APPOINTMENT	MEAL PLAN
☐	☐
☐	☐
☐	☐
☐	☐

FINANCIAL GOAL	WATER INTAKE
☐	☐
☐	☐
☐	☐
☐	☐

POSITIVE MOMENT	NOTE

MOTIVATION PLAN

DATE: _____   M T W TH F SA SU

TO DO
- ☐ ....
- ☐ ....
- ☐ ....
- ☐ ....

WORKOUT
- ☐ ....
- ☐ ....
- ☐ ....
- ☐ ....

APPOINTMENT
- ☐ ....
- ☐ ....
- ☐ ....
- ☐ ....

MEAL PLAN
- ☐ ....
- ☐ ....
- ☐ ....
- ☐ ....

FINANCIAL GOAL
- ☐ ....
- ☐ ....
- ☐ ....
- ☐ ....

WATER INTAKE
- ☐ ....
- ☐ ....
- ☐ ....
- ☐ ....

POSITIVE MOMENT
....
....
....
....

NOTE
....
....
....
....

MOTIVATION PLAN

DATE: _____   M   T   W   TH   F   SA   SU

TO DO

- [ ]
- [ ]
- [ ]
- [ ]

WORKOUT

- [ ]
- [ ]
- [ ]
- [ ]

APPOINTMENT

- [ ]
- [ ]
- [ ]
- [ ]

MEAL PLAN

- [ ]
- [ ]
- [ ]
- [ ]

FINANCIAL GOAL

- [ ]
- [ ]
- [ ]
- [ ]

WATER INTAKE

- [ ]
- [ ]
- [ ]
- [ ]

POSITIVE MOMENT

NOTE

MOTIVATION PLAN

DATE: _____

M T W TH F SA SU

TO DO

- [ ] ....
- [ ] ....
- [ ] ....
- [ ] ....

WORKOUT

- [ ] ....
- [ ] ....
- [ ] ....
- [ ] ....

APPOINTMENT

- [ ] ....
- [ ] ....
- [ ] ....
- [ ] ....

MEAL PLAN

- [ ] ....
- [ ] ....
- [ ] ....
- [ ] ....

FINANCIAL GOAL

- [ ] ....
- [ ] ....
- [ ] ....
- [ ] ....

WATER INTAKE

- [ ] ....
- [ ] ....
- [ ] ....
- [ ] ....

POSITIVE MOMENT

....
....
....
....

NOTE

....
....
....
....

MOTIVATION PLAN

DATE: _____   M T W TH F SA SU

TO DO
- ☐ ....
- ☐ ....
- ☐ ....
- ☐ ....

WORKOUT
- ☐ ....
- ☐ ....
- ☐ ....
- ☐ ....

APPOINTMENT
- ☐ ....
- ☐ ....
- ☐ ....
- ☐ ....

MEAL PLAN
- ☐ ....
- ☐ ....
- ☐ ....
- ☐ ....

FINANCIAL GOAL
- ☐ ....
- ☐ ....
- ☐ ....
- ☐ ....

WATER INTAKE
- ☐ ....
- ☐ ....
- ☐ ....
- ☐ ....

POSITIVE MOMENT
....
....
....
....

NOTE
....
....
....
....

MOTIVATION PLAN

DATE: _____

M T W TH F SA SU

TO DO
- [ ] ....
- [ ] ....
- [ ] ....
- [ ] ....

WORKOUT
- [ ] ....
- [ ] ....
- [ ] ....
- [ ] ....

APPOINTMENT
- [ ] ....
- [ ] ....
- [ ] ....
- [ ] ....

MEAL PLAN
- [ ] ....
- [ ] ....
- [ ] ....
- [ ] ....

FINANCIAL GOAL
- [ ] ....
- [ ] ....
- [ ] ....
- [ ] ....

WATER INTAKE
- [ ] ....
- [ ] ....
- [ ] ....
- [ ] ....

POSITIVE MOMENT
....
....
....
....

NOTE
....
....
....
....

MOTIVATION PLAN

DATE: _____   M   T   W   TH   F   SA   SU

TO DO
- [ ] ....
- [ ] ....
- [ ] ....
- [ ] ....

WORKOUT
- [ ] ....
- [ ] ....
- [ ] ....
- [ ] ....

APPOINTMENT
- [ ] ....
- [ ] ....
- [ ] ....
- [ ] ....

MEAL PLAN
- [ ] ....
- [ ] ....
- [ ] ....
- [ ] ....

FINANCIAL GOAL
- [ ] ....
- [ ] ....
- [ ] ....
- [ ] ....

WATER INTAKE
- [ ] ....
- [ ] ....
- [ ] ....
- [ ] ....

POSITIVE MOMENT
....
....
....
....

NOTE
....
....
....
....

MOTIVATION PLAN

DATE: _____   M T W TH F SA SU

TO DO
- ☐ ....
- ☐ ....
- ☐ ....
- ☐ ....

WORKOUT
- ☐ ....
- ☐ ....
- ☐ ....
- ☐ ....

APPOINTMENT
- ☐ ....
- ☐ ....
- ☐ ....
- ☐ ....

MEAL PLAN
- ☐ ....
- ☐ ....
- ☐ ....
- ☐ ....

FINANCIAL GOAL
- ☐ ....
- ☐ ....
- ☐ ....
- ☐ ....

WATER INTAKE
- ☐ ....
- ☐ ....
- ☐ ....
- ☐ ....

POSITIVE MOMENT
....
....
....
....

NOTE
....
....
....
....

MOTIVATION PLAN

DATE: _____   M   T   W   TH   F   SA   SU

TO DO
- ☐
- ☐
- ☐
- ☐

WORKOUT
- ☐
- ☐
- ☐
- ☐

APPOINTMENT
- ☐
- ☐
- ☐
- ☐

MEAL PLAN
- ☐
- ☐
- ☐
- ☐

FINANCIAL GOAL
- ☐
- ☐
- ☐
- ☐

WATER INTAKE
- ☐
- ☐
- ☐
- ☐

POSITIVE MOMENT

NOTE

MOTIVATION PLAN

DATE: _____   M T W TH F SA SU

TO DO
- ☐ ....
- ☐ ....
- ☐ ....
- ☐ ....

WORKOUT
- ☐ ....
- ☐ ....
- ☐ ....
- ☐ ....

APPOINTMENT
- ☐ ....
- ☐ ....
- ☐ ....
- ☐ ....

MEAL PLAN
- ☐ ....
- ☐ ....
- ☐ ....
- ☐ ....

FINANCIAL GOAL
- ☐ ....
- ☐ ....
- ☐ ....
- ☐ ....

WATER INTAKE
- ☐ ....
- ☐ ....
- ☐ ....
- ☐ ....

POSITIVE MOMENT
....
....
....
....

NOTE
....
....
....
....

MOTIVATION PLAN

DATE: _____

M T W TH F SA SU

TO DO
- [ ] ....
- [ ] ....
- [ ] ....
- [ ] ....

WORKOUT
- [ ] ....
- [ ] ....
- [ ] ....
- [ ] ....

APPOINTMENT
- [ ] ....
- [ ] ....
- [ ] ....
- [ ] ....

MEAL PLAN
- [ ] ....
- [ ] ....
- [ ] ....
- [ ] ....

FINANCIAL GOAL
- [ ] ....
- [ ] ....
- [ ] ....
- [ ] ....

WATER INTAKE
- [ ] ....
- [ ] ....
- [ ] ....
- [ ] ....

POSITIVE MOMENT
....
....
....
....

NOTE
....
....
....
....

MOTIVATION PLAN

DATE: _____   M T W TH F SA SU

TO DO
- ☐ ....
- ☐ ....
- ☐ ....
- ☐ ....

WORKOUT
- ☐ ....
- ☐ ....
- ☐ ....
- ☐ ....

APPOINTMENT
- ☐ ....
- ☐ ....
- ☐ ....
- ☐ ....

MEAL PLAN
- ☐ ....
- ☐ ....
- ☐ ....
- ☐ ....

FINANCIAL GOAL
- ☐ ....
- ☐ ....
- ☐ ....
- ☐ ....

WATER INTAKE
- ☐ ....
- ☐ ....
- ☐ ....
- ☐ ....

POSITIVE MOMENT
....
....
....
....

NOTE
....
....
....
....

MOTIVATION PLAN

DATE: _____

M T W TH F SA SU

TO DO
- [ ] ....
- [ ] ....
- [ ] ....
- [ ] ....

WORKOUT
- [ ] ....
- [ ] ....
- [ ] ....
- [ ] ....

APPOINTMENT
- [ ] ....
- [ ] ....
- [ ] ....
- [ ] ....

MEAL PLAN
- [ ] ....
- [ ] ....
- [ ] ....
- [ ] ....

FINANCIAL GOAL
- [ ] ....
- [ ] ....
- [ ] ....
- [ ] ....

WATER INTAKE
- [ ] ....
- [ ] ....
- [ ] ....
- [ ] ....

POSITIVE MOMENT
....
....
....
....

NOTE
....
....
....
....

MOTIVATION PLAN

DATE: _____   M T W TH F SA SU

TO DO

- [ ] ....
- [ ] ....
- [ ] ....
- [ ] ....

WORKOUT

- [ ] ....
- [ ] ....
- [ ] ....
- [ ] ....

APPOINTMENT

- [ ] ....
- [ ] ....
- [ ] ....
- [ ] ....

MEAL PLAN

- [ ] ....
- [ ] ....
- [ ] ....
- [ ] ....

FINANCIAL GOAL

- [ ] ....
- [ ] ....
- [ ] ....
- [ ] ....

WATER INTAKE

- [ ] ....
- [ ] ....
- [ ] ....
- [ ] ....

POSITIVE MOMENT

....
....
....
....

NOTE

....
....
....
....

MOTIVATION PLAN

DATE: _____   M T W TH F SA SU

TO DO
- [ ] ....
- [ ] ....
- [ ] ....
- [ ] ....

WORKOUT
- [ ] ....
- [ ] ....
- [ ] ....
- [ ] ....

APPOINTMENT
- [ ] ....
- [ ] ....
- [ ] ....
- [ ] ....

MEAL PLAN
- [ ] ....
- [ ] ....
- [ ] ....
- [ ] ....

FINANCIAL GOAL
- [ ] ....
- [ ] ....
- [ ] ....
- [ ] ....

WATER INTAKE
- [ ] ....
- [ ] ....
- [ ] ....
- [ ] ....

POSITIVE MOMENT
....
....
....
....

NOTE
....
....
....
....

MOTIVATION PLAN

DATE: _____   M T W TH F SA SU

TO DO

- [ ] ....
- [ ] ....
- [ ] ....
- [ ] ....

WORKOUT

- [ ] ....
- [ ] ....
- [ ] ....
- [ ] ....

APPOINTMENT

- [ ] ....
- [ ] ....
- [ ] ....
- [ ] ....

MEAL PLAN

- [ ] ....
- [ ] ....
- [ ] ....
- [ ] ....

FINANCIAL GOAL

- [ ] ....
- [ ] ....
- [ ] ....
- [ ] ....

WATER INTAKE

- [ ] ....
- [ ] ....
- [ ] ....
- [ ] ....

POSITIVE MOMENT

....
....
....
....

NOTE

....
....
....
....

MOTIVATION PLAN

DATE: _____   M T W TH F SA SU

TO DO
- ☐ ....
- ☐ ....
- ☐ ....
- ☐ ....

WORKOUT
- ☐ ....
- ☐ ....
- ☐ ....
- ☐ ....

APPOINTMENT
- ☐ ....
- ☐ ....
- ☐ ....
- ☐ ....

MEAL PLAN
- ☐ ....
- ☐ ....
- ☐ ....
- ☐ ....

FINANCIAL GOAL
- ☐ ....
- ☐ ....
- ☐ ....
- ☐ ....

WATER INTAKE
- ☐ ....
- ☐ ....
- ☐ ....
- ☐ ....

POSITIVE MOMENT
....
....
....
....

NOTE
....
....
....
....

MOTIVATION PLAN

DATE: _____   M   T   W   TH   F   SA   SU

TO DO

- ☐ ....
- ☐ ....
- ☐ ....
- ☐ ....

WORKOUT

- ☐ ....
- ☐ ....
- ☐ ....
- ☐ ....

APPOINTMENT

- ☐ ....
- ☐ ....
- ☐ ....
- ☐ ....

MEAL PLAN

- ☐ ....
- ☐ ....
- ☐ ....
- ☐ ....

FINANCIAL GOAL

- ☐ ....
- ☐ ....
- ☐ ....
- ☐ ....

WATER INTAKE

- ☐ ....
- ☐ ....
- ☐ ....
- ☐ ....

POSITIVE MOMENT

....
....
....
....

NOTE

....
....
....
....

MOTIVATION PLAN

DATE: _____   M T W TH F SA SU

TO DO
- [ ] ....
- [ ] ....
- [ ] ....
- [ ] ....

WORKOUT
- [ ] ....
- [ ] ....
- [ ] ....
- [ ] ....

APPOINTMENT
- [ ] ....
- [ ] ....
- [ ] ....
- [ ] ....

MEAL PLAN
- [ ] ....
- [ ] ....
- [ ] ....
- [ ] ....

FINANCIAL GOAL
- [ ] ....
- [ ] ....
- [ ] ....
- [ ] ....

WATER INTAKE
- [ ] ....
- [ ] ....
- [ ] ....
- [ ] ....

POSITIVE MOMENT
....
....
....
....

NOTE
....
....
....
....

MOTIVATION PLAN

DATE: _____   M T W TH F SA SU

TO DO

- [ ] ....
- [ ] ....
- [ ] ....
- [ ] ....

WORKOUT

- [ ] ....
- [ ] ....
- [ ] ....
- [ ] ....

APPOINTMENT

- [ ] ....
- [ ] ....
- [ ] ....
- [ ] ....

MEAL PLAN

- [ ] ....
- [ ] ....
- [ ] ....
- [ ] ....

FINANCIAL GOAL

- [ ] ....
- [ ] ....
- [ ] ....
- [ ] ....

WATER INTAKE

- [ ] ....
- [ ] ....
- [ ] ....
- [ ] ....

POSITIVE MOMENT

....
....
....
....

NOTE

....
....
....
....

MOTIVATION PLAN

DATE: _____   M T W TH F SA SU

TO DO
- [ ] ....
- [ ] ....
- [ ] ....
- [ ] ....

WORKOUT
- [ ] ....
- [ ] ....
- [ ] ....
- [ ] ....

APPOINTMENT
- [ ] ....
- [ ] ....
- [ ] ....
- [ ] ....

MEAL PLAN
- [ ] ....
- [ ] ....
- [ ] ....
- [ ] ....

FINANCIAL GOAL
- [ ] ....
- [ ] ....
- [ ] ....
- [ ] ....

WATER INTAKE
- [ ] ....
- [ ] ....
- [ ] ....
- [ ] ....

POSITIVE MOMENT
....
....
....
....

NOTE
....
....
....
....

MOTIVATION PLAN

DATE: _____   M T W TH F SA SU

TO DO
- [ ] ....
- [ ] ....
- [ ] ....
- [ ] ....

WORKOUT
- [ ] ....
- [ ] ....
- [ ] ....
- [ ] ....

APPOINTMENT
- [ ] ....
- [ ] ....
- [ ] ....
- [ ] ....

MEAL PLAN
- [ ] ....
- [ ] ....
- [ ] ....
- [ ] ....

FINANCIAL GOAL
- [ ] ....
- [ ] ....
- [ ] ....
- [ ] ....

WATER INTAKE
- [ ] ....
- [ ] ....
- [ ] ....
- [ ] ....

POSITIVE MOMENT
....
....
....
....

NOTE
....
....
....
....

MOTIVATION PLAN

DATE: _____   M T W TH F SA SU

TO DO
- [ ] ....
- [ ] ....
- [ ] ....
- [ ] ....

WORKOUT
- [ ] ....
- [ ] ....
- [ ] ....
- [ ] ....

APPOINTMENT
- [ ] ....
- [ ] ....
- [ ] ....
- [ ] ....

MEAL PLAN
- [ ] ....
- [ ] ....
- [ ] ....
- [ ] ....

FINANCIAL GOAL
- [ ] ....
- [ ] ....
- [ ] ....
- [ ] ....

WATER INTAKE
- [ ] ....
- [ ] ....
- [ ] ....
- [ ] ....

POSITIVE MOMENT
....
....
....
....

NOTE
....
....
....
....

MOTIVATION PLAN

DATE: _____   M T W TH F SA SU

TO DO
- [ ] ....
- [ ] ....
- [ ] ....
- [ ] ....

WORKOUT
- [ ] ....
- [ ] ....
- [ ] ....
- [ ] ....

APPOINTMENT
- [ ] ....
- [ ] ....
- [ ] ....
- [ ] ....

MEAL PLAN
- [ ] ....
- [ ] ....
- [ ] ....
- [ ] ....

FINANCIAL GOAL
- [ ] ....
- [ ] ....
- [ ] ....
- [ ] ....

WATER INTAKE
- [ ] ....
- [ ] ....
- [ ] ....
- [ ] ....

POSITIVE MOMENT
....
....
....
....

NOTE
....
....
....
....

MOTIVATION PLAN

DATE: _____   M T W TH F SA SU

TO DO

☐ ....

☐ ....

☐ ....

☐ ....

WORKOUT

☐ ....

☐ ....

☐ ....

☐ ....

APPOINTMENT

☐ ....

☐ ....

☐ ....

☐ ....

MEAL PLAN

☐ ....

☐ ....

☐ ....

☐ ....

FINANCIAL GOAL

☐ ....

☐ ....

☐ ....

☐ ....

WATER INTAKE

☐ ....

☐ ....

☐ ....

☐ ....

POSITIVE MOMENT

....

....

....

....

NOTE

....

....

....

....

MOTIVATION PLAN

DATE: _____   M T W TH F SA SU

TO DO
- ☐ ....
- ☐ ....
- ☐ ....
- ☐ ....

WORKOUT
- ☐ ....
- ☐ ....
- ☐ ....
- ☐ ....

APPOINTMENT
- ☐ ....
- ☐ ....
- ☐ ....
- ☐ ....

MEAL PLAN
- ☐ ....
- ☐ ....
- ☐ ....
- ☐ ....

FINANCIAL GOAL
- ☐ ....
- ☐ ....
- ☐ ....
- ☐ ....

WATER INTAKE
- ☐ ....
- ☐ ....
- ☐ ....
- ☐ ....

POSITIVE MOMENT
....
....
....
....

NOTE
....
....
....
....

MOTIVATION PLAN

DATE: _____   M T W TH F SA SU

TO DO

- [ ] ....
- [ ] ....
- [ ] ....
- [ ] ....

WORKOUT

- [ ] ....
- [ ] ....
- [ ] ....
- [ ] ....

APPOINTMENT

- [ ] ....
- [ ] ....
- [ ] ....
- [ ] ....

MEAL PLAN

- [ ] ....
- [ ] ....
- [ ] ....
- [ ] ....

FINANCIAL GOAL

- [ ] ....
- [ ] ....
- [ ] ....
- [ ] ....

WATER INTAKE

- [ ] ....
- [ ] ....
- [ ] ....
- [ ] ....

POSITIVE MOMENT

....
....
....
....

NOTE

....
....
....
....

MOTIVATION PLAN

DATE: _____

M T W TH F SA SU

TO DO

- [ ] ....
- [ ] ....
- [ ] ....
- [ ] ....

WORKOUT

- [ ] ....
- [ ] ....
- [ ] ....
- [ ] ....

APPOINTMENT

- [ ] ....
- [ ] ....
- [ ] ....
- [ ] ....

MEAL PLAN

- [ ] ....
- [ ] ....
- [ ] ....
- [ ] ....

FINANCIAL GOAL

- [ ] ....
- [ ] ....
- [ ] ....
- [ ] ....

WATER INTAKE

- [ ] ....
- [ ] ....
- [ ] ....
- [ ] ....

POSITIVE MOMENT

....
....
....
....

NOTE

....
....
....
....

MOTIVATION PLAN

DATE: _____   M T W TH F SA SU

TO DO
- [ ] ....
- [ ] ....
- [ ] ....
- [ ] ....

WORKOUT
- [ ] ....
- [ ] ....
- [ ] ....
- [ ] ....

APPOINTMENT
- [ ] ....
- [ ] ....
- [ ] ....
- [ ] ....

MEAL PLAN
- [ ] ....
- [ ] ....
- [ ] ....
- [ ] ....

FINANCIAL GOAL
- [ ] ....
- [ ] ....
- [ ] ....
- [ ] ....

WATER INTAKE
- [ ] ....
- [ ] ....
- [ ] ....
- [ ] ....

POSITIVE MOMENT
....
....
....
....

NOTE
....
....
....
....

MOTIVATION PLAN

DATE: _____   M T W TH F SA SU

TO DO

- [ ] ....
- [ ] ....
- [ ] ....
- [ ] ....

WORKOUT

- [ ] ....
- [ ] ....
- [ ] ....
- [ ] ....

APPOINTMENT

- [ ] ....
- [ ] ....
- [ ] ....
- [ ] ....

MEAL PLAN

- [ ] ....
- [ ] ....
- [ ] ....
- [ ] ....

FINANCIAL GOAL

- [ ] ....
- [ ] ....
- [ ] ....
- [ ] ....

WATER INTAKE

- [ ] ....
- [ ] ....
- [ ] ....
- [ ] ....

POSITIVE MOMENT

....
....
....
....

NOTE

....
....
....
....

MOTIVATION PLAN

DATE: _____   M   T   W   TH   F   SA   SU

TO DO
- [ ] ....
- [ ] ....
- [ ] ....
- [ ] ....

WORKOUT
- [ ] ....
- [ ] ....
- [ ] ....
- [ ] ....

APPOINTMENT
- [ ] ....
- [ ] ....
- [ ] ....
- [ ] ....

MEAL PLAN
- [ ] ....
- [ ] ....
- [ ] ....
- [ ] ....

FINANCIAL GOAL
- [ ] ....
- [ ] ....
- [ ] ....
- [ ] ....

WATER INTAKE
- [ ] ....
- [ ] ....
- [ ] ....
- [ ] ....

POSITIVE MOMENT
....
....
....
....

NOTE
....
....
....
....

MOTIVATION PLAN

DATE: _____   M T W TH F SA SU

TO DO

- ☐ ....
- ☐ ....
- ☐ ....
- ☐ ....

WORKOUT

- ☐ ....
- ☐ ....
- ☐ ....
- ☐ ....

APPOINTMENT

- ☐ ....
- ☐ ....
- ☐ ....
- ☐ ....

MEAL PLAN

- ☐ ....
- ☐ ....
- ☐ ....
- ☐ ....

FINANCIAL GOAL

- ☐ ....
- ☐ ....
- ☐ ....
- ☐ ....

WATER INTAKE

- ☐ ....
- ☐ ....
- ☐ ....
- ☐ ....

POSITIVE MOMENT

....
....
....
....

NOTE

....
....
....
....

MOTIVATION PLAN

DATE: _____   M T W TH F SA SU

TO DO
- ☐ ....
- ☐ ....
- ☐ ....
- ☐ ....

WORKOUT
- ☐ ....
- ☐ ....
- ☐ ....
- ☐ ....

APPOINTMENT
- ☐ ....
- ☐ ....
- ☐ ....
- ☐ ....

MEAL PLAN
- ☐ ....
- ☐ ....
- ☐ ....
- ☐ ....

FINANCIAL GOAL
- ☐ ....
- ☐ ....
- ☐ ....
- ☐ ....

WATER INTAKE
- ☐ ....
- ☐ ....
- ☐ ....
- ☐ ....

POSITIVE MOMENT
....
....
....
....

NOTE
....
....
....
....

MOTIVATION PLAN

DATE: _____   M T W TH F SA SU

TO DO
- [ ] ....
- [ ] ....
- [ ] ....
- [ ] ....

WORKOUT
- [ ] ....
- [ ] ....
- [ ] ....
- [ ] ....

APPOINTMENT
- [ ] ....
- [ ] ....
- [ ] ....
- [ ] ....

MEAL PLAN
- [ ] ....
- [ ] ....
- [ ] ....
- [ ] ....

FINANCIAL GOAL
- [ ] ....
- [ ] ....
- [ ] ....
- [ ] ....

WATER INTAKE
- [ ] ....
- [ ] ....
- [ ] ....
- [ ] ....

POSITIVE MOMENT
....
....
....
....

NOTE
....
....
....
....

MOTIVATION PLAN

DATE: _____   M T W TH F SA SU

TO DO

☐ ....

☐ ....

☐ ....

☐ ....

APPOINTMENT

☐ ....

☐ ....

☐ ....

☐ ....

FINANCIAL GOAL

☐ ....

☐ ....

☐ ....

☐ ....

POSITIVE MOMENT

....

....

....

....

WORKOUT

☐ ....

☐ ....

☐ ....

☐ ....

MEAL PLAN

☐ ....

☐ ....

☐ ....

☐ ....

WATER INTAKE

☐ ....

☐ ....

☐ ....

☐ ....

NOTE

....

....

....

....

MOTIVATION PLAN

DATE: _____   M T W TH F SA SU

TO DO

☐ ....
☐ ....
☐ ....
☐ ....

WORKOUT

☐ ....
☐ ....
☐ ....
☐ ....

APPOINTMENT

☐ ....
☐ ....
☐ ....
☐ ....

MEAL PLAN

☐ ....
☐ ....
☐ ....
☐ ....

FINANCIAL GOAL

☐ ....
☐ ....
☐ ....
☐ ....

WATER INTAKE

☐ ....
☐ ....
☐ ....
☐ ....

POSITIVE MOMENT

....
....
....
....

NOTE

....
....
....
....

MOTIVATION PLAN

DATE: _____   M T W TH F SA SU

TO DO
- ☐ ....
- ☐ ....
- ☐ ....
- ☐ ....

WORKOUT
- ☐ ....
- ☐ ....
- ☐ ....
- ☐ ....

APPOINTMENT
- ☐ ....
- ☐ ....
- ☐ ....
- ☐ ....

MEAL PLAN
- ☐ ....
- ☐ ....
- ☐ ....
- ☐ ....

FINANCIAL GOAL
- ☐ ....
- ☐ ....
- ☐ ....
- ☐ ....

WATER INTAKE
- ☐ ....
- ☐ ....
- ☐ ....
- ☐ ....

POSITIVE MOMENT
....
....
....
....

NOTE
....
....
....
....

MOTIVATION PLAN

DATE: _____   M T W TH F SA SU

TO DO

- ☐ ....
- ☐ ....
- ☐ ....
- ☐ ....

WORKOUT

- ☐ ....
- ☐ ....
- ☐ ....
- ☐ ....

APPOINTMENT

- ☐ ....
- ☐ ....
- ☐ ....
- ☐ ....

MEAL PLAN

- ☐ ....
- ☐ ....
- ☐ ....
- ☐ ....

FINANCIAL GOAL

- ☐ ....
- ☐ ....
- ☐ ....
- ☐ ....

WATER INTAKE

- ☐ ....
- ☐ ....
- ☐ ....
- ☐ ....

POSITIVE MOMENT

....
....
....
....

NOTE

....
....
....
....

MOTIVATION PLAN

DATE: _____

M T W TH F SA SU

TO DO

- ☐ ....
- ☐ ....
- ☐ ....
- ☐ ....

WORKOUT

- ☐ ....
- ☐ ....
- ☐ ....
- ☐ ....

APPOINTMENT

- ☐ ....
- ☐ ....
- ☐ ....
- ☐ ....

MEAL PLAN

- ☐ ....
- ☐ ....
- ☐ ....
- ☐ ....

FINANCIAL GOAL

- ☐ ....
- ☐ ....
- ☐ ....
- ☐ ....

WATER INTAKE

- ☐ ....
- ☐ ....
- ☐ ....
- ☐ ....

POSITIVE MOMENT

....
....
....
....

NOTE

....
....
....
....

MOTIVATION PLAN

DATE: _____   M T W TH F SA SU

TO DO

- [ ] ....
- [ ] ....
- [ ] ....
- [ ] ....

WORKOUT

- [ ] ....
- [ ] ....
- [ ] ....
- [ ] ....

APPOINTMENT

- [ ] ....
- [ ] ....
- [ ] ....
- [ ] ....

MEAL PLAN

- [ ] ....
- [ ] ....
- [ ] ....
- [ ] ....

FINANCIAL GOAL

- [ ] ....
- [ ] ....
- [ ] ....
- [ ] ....

WATER INTAKE

- [ ] ....
- [ ] ....
- [ ] ....
- [ ] ....

POSITIVE MOMENT

....
....
....
....

NOTE

....
....
....
....

MOTIVATION PLAN

DATE: _____   M T W TH F SA SU

TO DO

- [ ]
- [ ]
- [ ]
- [ ]

WORKOUT

- [ ]
- [ ]
- [ ]
- [ ]

APPOINTMENT

- [ ]
- [ ]
- [ ]
- [ ]

MEAL PLAN

- [ ]
- [ ]
- [ ]
- [ ]

FINANCIAL GOAL

- [ ]
- [ ]
- [ ]
- [ ]

WATER INTAKE

- [ ]
- [ ]
- [ ]
- [ ]

POSITIVE MOMENT

NOTE

MOTIVATION PLAN

DATE: _____   M T W TH F SA SU

TO DO

- [ ] ....
- [ ] ....
- [ ] ....
- [ ] ....

WORKOUT

- [ ] ....
- [ ] ....
- [ ] ....
- [ ] ....

APPOINTMENT

- [ ] ....
- [ ] ....
- [ ] ....
- [ ] ....

MEAL PLAN

- [ ] ....
- [ ] ....
- [ ] ....
- [ ] ....

FINANCIAL GOAL

- [ ] ....
- [ ] ....
- [ ] ....
- [ ] ....

WATER INTAKE

- [ ] ....
- [ ] ....
- [ ] ....
- [ ] ....

POSITIVE MOMENT

....
....
....
....

NOTE

....
....
....
....

MOTIVATION PLAN

DATE: _____   M T W TH F SA SU

TO DO

- ☐ ....
- ☐ ....
- ☐ ....
- ☐ ....

WORKOUT

- ☐ ....
- ☐ ....
- ☐ ....
- ☐ ....

APPOINTMENT

- ☐ ....
- ☐ ....
- ☐ ....
- ☐ ....

MEAL PLAN

- ☐ ....
- ☐ ....
- ☐ ....
- ☐ ....

FINANCIAL GOAL

- ☐ ....
- ☐ ....
- ☐ ....
- ☐ ....

WATER INTAKE

- ☐ ....
- ☐ ....
- ☐ ....
- ☐ ....

POSITIVE MOMENT

....
....
....
....

NOTE

....
....
....
....

MOTIVATION PLAN

DATE: _____   M T W TH F SA SU

TO DO
- ☐ ....
- ☐ ....
- ☐ ....
- ☐ ....

WORKOUT
- ☐ ....
- ☐ ....
- ☐ ....
- ☐ ....

APPOINTMENT
- ☐ ....
- ☐ ....
- ☐ ....
- ☐ ....

MEAL PLAN
- ☐ ....
- ☐ ....
- ☐ ....
- ☐ ....

FINANCIAL GOAL
- ☐ ....
- ☐ ....
- ☐ ....
- ☐ ....

WATER INTAKE
- ☐ ....
- ☐ ....
- ☐ ....
- ☐ ....

POSITIVE MOMENT
....
....
....
....

NOTE
....
....
....
....

MOTIVATION PLAN

DATE: _____   M T W TH F SA SU

TO DO

- ☐ ....
- ☐ ....
- ☐ ....
- ☐ ....

WORKOUT

- ☐ ....
- ☐ ....
- ☐ ....
- ☐ ....

APPOINTMENT

- ☐ ....
- ☐ ....
- ☐ ....
- ☐ ....

MEAL PLAN

- ☐ ....
- ☐ ....
- ☐ ....
- ☐ ....

FINANCIAL GOAL

- ☐ ....
- ☐ ....
- ☐ ....
- ☐ ....

WATER INTAKE

- ☐ ....
- ☐ ....
- ☐ ....
- ☐ ....

POSITIVE MOMENT

....
....
....
....

NOTE

....
....
....
....

MOTIVATION PLAN

DATE: _____   M   T   W   TH   F   SA   SU

TO DO

- [ ] ....
- [ ] ....
- [ ] ....
- [ ] ....

WORKOUT

- [ ] ....
- [ ] ....
- [ ] ....
- [ ] ....

APPOINTMENT

- [ ] ....
- [ ] ....
- [ ] ....
- [ ] ....

MEAL PLAN

- [ ] ....
- [ ] ....
- [ ] ....
- [ ] ....

FINANCIAL GOAL

- [ ] ....
- [ ] ....
- [ ] ....
- [ ] ....

WATER INTAKE

- [ ] ....
- [ ] ....
- [ ] ....
- [ ] ....

POSITIVE MOMENT

....
....
....
....

NOTE

....
....
....
....

MOTIVATION PLAN

DATE: _____   M T W TH F SA SU

TO DO
- [ ]
- [ ]
- [ ]
- [ ]

WORKOUT
- [ ]
- [ ]
- [ ]
- [ ]

APPOINTMENT
- [ ]
- [ ]
- [ ]
- [ ]

MEAL PLAN
- [ ]
- [ ]
- [ ]
- [ ]

FINANCIAL GOAL
- [ ]
- [ ]
- [ ]
- [ ]

WATER INTAKE
- [ ]
- [ ]
- [ ]
- [ ]

POSITIVE MOMENT

NOTE

MOTIVATION PLAN

DATE: _____   M T W TH F SA SU

TO DO
- ☐ ....
- ☐ ....
- ☐ ....
- ☐ ....

WORKOUT
- ☐ ....
- ☐ ....
- ☐ ....
- ☐ ....

APPOINTMENT
- ☐ ....
- ☐ ....
- ☐ ....
- ☐ ....

MEAL PLAN
- ☐ ....
- ☐ ....
- ☐ ....
- ☐ ....

FINANCIAL GOAL
- ☐ ....
- ☐ ....
- ☐ ....
- ☐ ....

WATER INTAKE
- ☐ ....
- ☐ ....
- ☐ ....
- ☐ ....

POSITIVE MOMENT
....
....
....
....

NOTE
....
....
....
....

MOTIVATION PLAN

DATE: _____   M   T   W   TH   F   SA   SU

TO DO

☐ ....
☐ ....
☐ ....
☐ ....

WORKOUT

☐ ....
☐ ....
☐ ....
☐ ....

APPOINTMENT

☐ ....
☐ ....
☐ ....
☐ ....

MEAL PLAN

☐ ....
☐ ....
☐ ....
☐ ....

FINANCIAL GOAL

☐ ....
☐ ....
☐ ....
☐ ....

WATER INTAKE

☐ ....
☐ ....
☐ ....
☐ ....

POSITIVE MOMENT

....
....
....
....

NOTE

....
....
....
....

MOTIVATION PLAN

DATE: _____   M T W TH F SA SU

TO DO

☐ ....
☐ ....
☐ ....
☐ ....

WORKOUT

☐ ....
☐ ....
☐ ....
☐ ....

APPOINTMENT

☐ ....
☐ ....
☐ ....
☐ ....

MEAL PLAN

☐ ....
☐ ....
☐ ....
☐ ....

FINANCIAL GOAL

☐ ....
☐ ....
☐ ....
☐ ....

WATER INTAKE

☐ ....
☐ ....
☐ ....
☐ ....

POSITIVE MOMENT

....
....
....
....

NOTE

....
....
....
....

MOTIVATION PLAN

DATE: _____   M   T   W   TH   F   SA   SU

TO DO

- ☐ ....
- ☐ ....
- ☐ ....
- ☐ ....

WORKOUT

- ☐ ....
- ☐ ....
- ☐ ....
- ☐ ....

APPOINTMENT

- ☐ ....
- ☐ ....
- ☐ ....
- ☐ ....

MEAL PLAN

- ☐ ....
- ☐ ....
- ☐ ....
- ☐ ....

FINANCIAL GOAL

- ☐ ....
- ☐ ....
- ☐ ....
- ☐ ....

WATER INTAKE

- ☐ ....
- ☐ ....
- ☐ ....
- ☐ ....

POSITIVE MOMENT

....
....
....
....

NOTE

....
....
....
....

MOTIVATION PLAN

DATE: _____   M T W TH F SA SU

TO DO
- [ ] ....
- [ ] ....
- [ ] ....
- [ ] ....

WORKOUT
- [ ] ....
- [ ] ....
- [ ] ....
- [ ] ....

APPOINTMENT
- [ ] ....
- [ ] ....
- [ ] ....
- [ ] ....

MEAL PLAN
- [ ] ....
- [ ] ....
- [ ] ....
- [ ] ....

FINANCIAL GOAL
- [ ] ....
- [ ] ....
- [ ] ....
- [ ] ....

WATER INTAKE
- [ ] ....
- [ ] ....
- [ ] ....
- [ ] ....

POSITIVE MOMENT
....
....
....
....

NOTE
....
....
....
....

MOTIVATION PLAN

DATE: _____   M T W TH F SA SU

TO DO
- [ ] ....
- [ ] ....
- [ ] ....
- [ ] ....

WORKOUT
- [ ] ....
- [ ] ....
- [ ] ....
- [ ] ....

APPOINTMENT
- [ ] ....
- [ ] ....
- [ ] ....
- [ ] ....

MEAL PLAN
- [ ] ....
- [ ] ....
- [ ] ....
- [ ] ....

FINANCIAL GOAL
- [ ] ....
- [ ] ....
- [ ] ....
- [ ] ....

WATER INTAKE
- [ ] ....
- [ ] ....
- [ ] ....
- [ ] ....

POSITIVE MOMENT
....
....
....
....

NOTE
....
....
....
....

MOTIVATION PLAN

DATE: _____   M T W TH F SA SU

TO DO
- ☐ ....
- ☐ ....
- ☐ ....
- ☐ ....

WORKOUT
- ☐ ....
- ☐ ....
- ☐ ....
- ☐ ....

APPOINTMENT
- ☐ ....
- ☐ ....
- ☐ ....
- ☐ ....

MEAL PLAN
- ☐ ....
- ☐ ....
- ☐ ....
- ☐ ....

FINANCIAL GOAL
- ☐ ....
- ☐ ....
- ☐ ....
- ☐ ....

WATER INTAKE
- ☐ ....
- ☐ ....
- ☐ ....
- ☐ ....

POSITIVE MOMENT
....
....
....
....

NOTE
....
....
....
....

MOTIVATION PLAN

DATE: _____   M T W TH F SA SU

TO DO
- ☐ ....
- ☐ ....
- ☐ ....
- ☐ ....

WORKOUT
- ☐ ....
- ☐ ....
- ☐ ....
- ☐ ....

APPOINTMENT
- ☐ ....
- ☐ ....
- ☐ ....
- ☐ ....

MEAL PLAN
- ☐ ....
- ☐ ....
- ☐ ....
- ☐ ....

FINANCIAL GOAL
- ☐ ....
- ☐ ....
- ☐ ....
- ☐ ....

WATER INTAKE
- ☐ ....
- ☐ ....
- ☐ ....
- ☐ ....

POSITIVE MOMENT
....
....
....
....

NOTE
....
....
....
....

MOTIVATION PLAN

DATE: _____

M T W TH F SA SU

TO DO
- [ ] ....
- [ ] ....
- [ ] ....
- [ ] ....

WORKOUT
- [ ] ....
- [ ] ....
- [ ] ....
- [ ] ....

APPOINTMENT
- [ ] ....
- [ ] ....
- [ ] ....
- [ ] ....

MEAL PLAN
- [ ] ....
- [ ] ....
- [ ] ....
- [ ] ....

FINANCIAL GOAL
- [ ] ....
- [ ] ....
- [ ] ....
- [ ] ....

WATER INTAKE
- [ ] ....
- [ ] ....
- [ ] ....
- [ ] ....

POSITIVE MOMENT
....
....
....
....

NOTE
....
....
....
....

MOTIVATION PLAN

DATE: _____   M T W TH F SA SU

TO DO
☐ ....
☐ ....
☐ ....
☐ ....

WORKOUT
☐ ....
☐ ....
☐ ....
☐ ....

APPOINTMENT
☐ ....
☐ ....
☐ ....
☐ ....

MEAL PLAN
☐ ....
☐ ....
☐ ....
☐ ....

FINANCIAL GOAL
☐ ....
☐ ....
☐ ....
☐ ....

WATER INTAKE
☐ ....
☐ ....
☐ ....
☐ ....

POSITIVE MOMENT
....
....
....
....

NOTE
....
....
....
....

MOTIVATION PLAN

DATE: _____   M T W TH F SA SU

TO DO

☐ ....
☐ ....
☐ ....
☐ ....

WORKOUT

☐ ....
☐ ....
☐ ....
☐ ....

APPOINTMENT

☐ ....
☐ ....
☐ ....
☐ ....

MEAL PLAN

☐ ....
☐ ....
☐ ....
☐ ....

FINANCIAL GOAL

☐ ....
☐ ....
☐ ....
☐ ....

WATER INTAKE

☐ ....
☐ ....
☐ ....
☐ ....

POSITIVE MOMENT

....
....
....
....

NOTE

....
....
....
....

MOTIVATION PLAN

DATE: _____   M T W TH F SA SU

TO DO
- [ ] ....
- [ ] ....
- [ ] ....
- [ ] ....

WORKOUT
- [ ] ....
- [ ] ....
- [ ] ....
- [ ] ....

APPOINTMENT
- [ ] ....
- [ ] ....
- [ ] ....
- [ ] ....

MEAL PLAN
- [ ] ....
- [ ] ....
- [ ] ....
- [ ] ....

FINANCIAL GOAL
- [ ] ....
- [ ] ....
- [ ] ....
- [ ] ....

WATER INTAKE
- [ ] ....
- [ ] ....
- [ ] ....
- [ ] ....

POSITIVE MOMENT
....
....
....
....

NOTE
....
....
....
....

Made in United States
Orlando, FL
25 January 2023